THE FOOD PYRAMID

A TRUE BOOK

by
Joan Kalbacken

Children's Press®
A Division of Grolier Publishing

New York London Hong Kong Sydney
Danbury, Connecticut

A grocery cart full of healthy food

Reading Consultant
Linda Cornwell
*Learning Resource Consultant
Indiana Department
of Education*

Subject Consultants
Sandy McGhee
*Coordinator—Special Programs
and*
Robin Bagwell
*Family Life/Nutrition
McLean County Cooperative
Extension Service of the
University of Illinois,
Urbana-Champaign*

Visit Children's Press on the Internet at:
http://publishing.grolier.com

Library of Congress Cataloging-in-Publication Data

Kalbacken, Joan.
   The food pyramid / by Joan Kalbacken.
     p.   cm. — (A True book)
   Includes bibliographical references and index.
   Summary: Introduces the food pyramid, describing each level in detail,
and discusses nutrition, serving sizes, snacking, and the benefits of
healthy eating.
   ISBN: 0-516-20756-3 (lib. bdg.)   0-516-26376-5 (pbk.)
   1. Nutrition—Juvenile literature. 2. Health—Juvenile literature.
[1. Nutrition. 2. Health.] I. Title. II. Series.
   TX355.K22 1998
   613.2—dc21
                                                            97-8229
                                                              CIP
                                                              AC

Contents

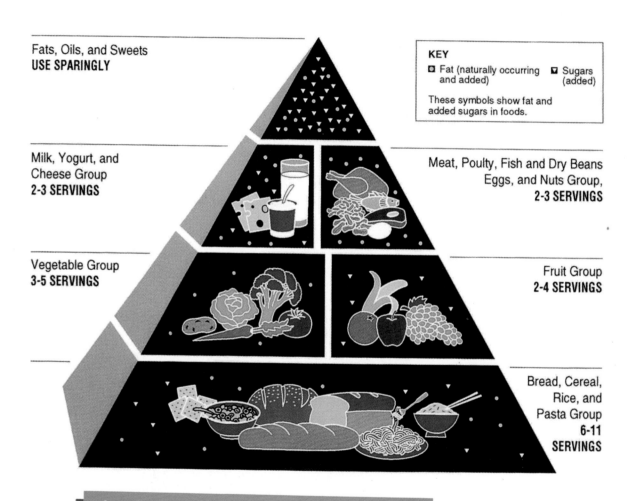

Fats, Oils, and Sweets
USE SPARINGLY

KEY
□ Fat (naturally occurring and added)   ▼ Sugars (added)
These symbols show fat and added sugars in foods.

Milk, Yogurt, and
Cheese Group
2-3 SERVINGS

Meat, Poulty, Fish and Dry Beans
Eggs, and Nuts Group,
2-3 SERVINGS

Vegetable Group
3-5 SERVINGS

Fruit Group
2-4 SERVINGS

Bread, Cereal,
Rice, and
Pasta Group
**6-11
SERVINGS**

The food pyramid was established
by the United States Department
of Agriculture (USDA).

The Food Pyramid

The food pyramid is a guide for good eating habits. It was developed to help people improve their health. The pyramid shows the right foods that both children and adults need to eat as part of a healthy diet. It also shows how much of each kind of food you should eat. The food pyramid is made up of food groups. Each group is important for good health.

The food pyramid has four different levels. There are five food groups shown in the first three levels of the pyramid. The food group at the bottom of the pyramid contains bread, cereal, rice, and pasta. The next level has two groups—vegetables and fruits. The third level also has two groups. One

What is a Pyramid?

A pyramid is a building or structure with a square base (bottom). It has four sloping sides. Each side is the shape of a triangle. The four sides meet at the top. A long time ago, kings in Egypt had pyramids built for their royal tombs. The pyramids of Egypt were used as models for the food pyramid.

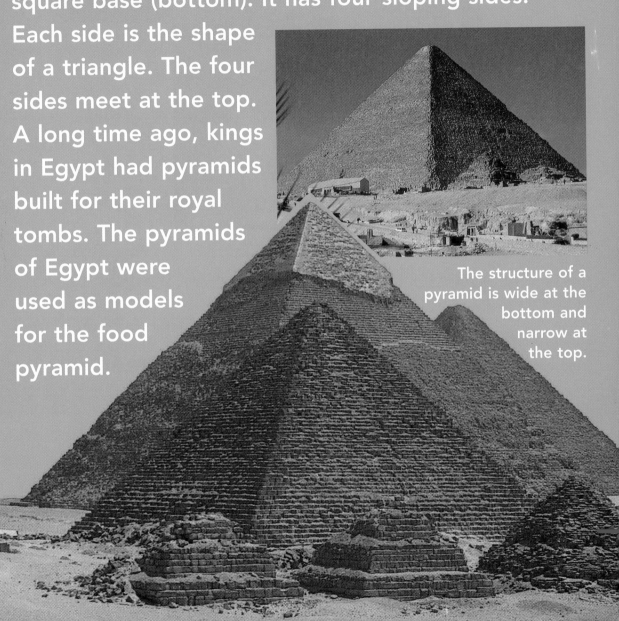

The structure of a pyramid is wide at the bottom and narrow at the top.

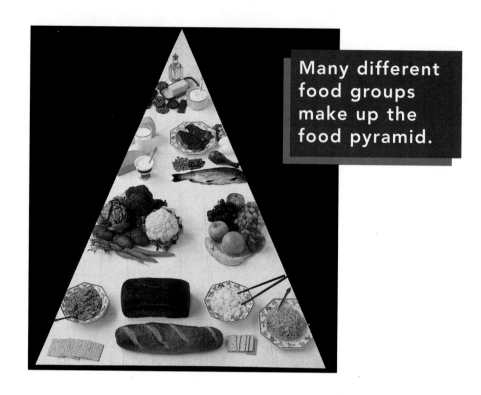

Many different food groups make up the food pyramid.

group includes dairy products such as milk, yogurt, and cheese. The other group includes meat, poultry (chicken or turkey), fish, dry beans, eggs, and nuts. The tiny group at the top contains fat, oil, and sugar.

Each of these food groups provides the nutrients you need for good health. Nutrients are parts of food that help you grow.

Eating the right foods helps you grow and keeps you healthy.

The Bottom Level

The bottom of the food pyramid is the biggest group. People need the most food from this group. Bread, cereal, rice, and pasta should make up a big part of everyone's diet each day. Foods such as macaroni and spaghetti are pasta. Cereals are made from many

These are some of the foods that are found in the group at the bottom of the pyramid.

different grains. Some of the grains are rye, wheat, oats, corn, and rice. Whole wheat crackers, oatmeal, and bran muffins are a few examples of grain foods.

11

The foods in this group give you vitamins and minerals that make you healthy. Vitamins and minerals are natural substances that are found in most foods. Vitamins and minerals help your body to grow healthy and strong. They also give you the energy you need each day. The foods at the bottom level of the food pyramid also contain fiber and starch. You need fiber because it helps food to

To be active like these kids, you need a lot of energy from the foods you eat.

move through your body.
Starch is important for energy
and strength.

The Second Level

The second level of the pyramid contains foods that come from plants. This group includes both vegetables and fruits. Vegetables contain a lot of vitamins. They also improve your eyesight. The vitamins in vegetables help to heal cuts and bruises. Like

The second level contains hundreds of tasty fruits and vegetables from all over the world.

the grain foods on the bottom level, vegetables contain fiber.

Vegetables come from different parts of plants. Some

vegetables you eat are from the stems, flowers, leaves, seeds, or even the roots of plants. Celery and asparagus are the stems of plants. The

The flower of the broccoli plant (below) is the part we usually eat. The part of the carrot that you eat is the root (right), which means it grows underground.

tops of broccoli or cauliflower are the flowers of plants. Lettuce and spinach are the leaves of plants. Carrots, beets, and radishes are the roots of plants. Beans and peas are plant seeds.

Fruits are found in the second level of the pyramid too. They also give you vitamins for growth and healthy skin. They help you to fight sickness. Fruits such as apples can even help you to clean your teeth!

Oranges, grapefruit, lemons, and limes are called citrus fruits. This special group of fruits contains a lot of vitamin C. Vitamin C is important because it fights diseases. If you do get sick, vitamin C helps you feel better faster. You can eat fruit that is fresh, canned, frozen, or dried. But fruit that is cut up, heated, frozen, or dried does not have as many vitamins as fresh fruit.

Fruits (below) work in a variety of ways to keep you healthy. Citrus fruits, such as these oranges (left), grow on trees or shrubs in areas called groves.

The Third Level

The third level of the pyramid has two food groups. One group is made up of meat, poultry, fish, dry beans, eggs, and nuts. The other group contains milk, yogurt, and cheese. These foods are called dairy products. Dairy products are important

The calcium that is found in dairy foods is important for both children and adults.

because they contain calcium. Calcium builds strong bones and healthy teeth.

The meat, poultry, fish, dry beans, eggs, and nuts group contains many different foods. That is because all the foods in this group contain some of the same nutrients. Most of the nutrients help to keep you healthy. But many of the foods in this group have a lot of fat in them. Your body needs a little fat to give you energy. Fat also keeps your body warm. But too much fat is unhealthy.

Although the nuts and red meat in this photo contain fat, they also contain important nutrients.

You should not eat too much of any of these foods.

The Top Level

The group at the top of the food pyramid is the smallest. This group contains fat, oil, and sugar. Potato chips, fried foods, candy, cake, ice cream, and cookies are found in this group. The food pyramid tells you to eat only small amounts of these foods, and not to eat

Many people enjoy eating food that is sweet or fattening, but too much of these foods can make you sick.

them very often. Most people enjoy eating foods with a lot of fat and sugar. In fact, many people's favorite foods are found in this group. But too much fat and sugar can cause diseases and obesity (being dangerously overweight). Fat, oil, and sugar have few nutrients that are needed for good health.

Some snacks are also found in this top level. But snacks that don't have a lot of fat or sugar can be important for your health. Snacks can help you have more energy. The size of a snack should be small. You should never eat a snack instead of a meal. Examples of healthy snacks are fresh fruit, air-popped popcorn, natural fruit

Many snacks, such as fresh vegetables, milk, cheese, or air-popped popcorn, are good for you.

juices, fresh vegetables, and yogurt. Snack mixes of wheat, rice, corn, and bran cereals are good for you. Adding pretzels or raisins to cereal mixes gives them an extra-sweet taste.

Healthy snacks can also be a combination of foods from the different food groups. Combine celery and peanut butter for a stuffed celery snack. Cereal and milk or cheese and whole grain bread make good snack foods, too.

Pyramid Food Groups

The levels of the food pyramid are different sizes. This is because each level shows the amount of food you should eat from the food groups.

The bottom level of the pyramid is the largest group. You need the most servings from this group. A serving is

Eating cereal is a good way to get enough of the grain foods located at the bottom of the food pyramid.

an amount of food that you eat. You should eat about six to eleven servings of grain foods every day. From the second level, you should eat three to five servings of vegetables.

And you should also eat two to four servings of fruit. You need two to three servings of the dairy products on the third level. You also need two

Fruit can taste delicious whether it's eaten by itself or as part of another meal.

Chickens, turkeys, ducks, and geese are included in the poultry group.

to three servings from the meat, fish, poultry, eggs, dry beans, and nut group.

Does this seem like a lot of food to eat every day? Six to eleven servings from the bread, cereal, rice, and pasta group may sound like a lot to eat. But it really isn't. One slice of bread is one serving. If you eat a whole sandwich for lunch, you have two servings

Sandwiches are a good way to eat more than one serving of food from several different groups.

This family is enjoying food from the grain group, the poultry group, and the vegetable group all in one meal.

from the bottom group. One slice of toast and a small bowl of cereal for breakfast also equals two servings. If you have pasta or a bowl of rice at dinner, you've added one to two more servings from this group.

The serving sizes in the second pyramid level also work this way. One orange, banana, or apple is one serving. If you fill a cup with fruit juice or vegetable juice, you

The apple this boy picks will count as one serving from the fruit and vegetable group.

Yogurt is a dairy product. But when it contains fruit, you also are eating a serving from the fruit group.

will have one serving from the fruit and vegetable group.

A container of yogurt or a carton of milk from your school cafeteria is one serving from the dairy products group. One slice of cheese also equals one serving. A hamburger, a chicken breast, or a tuna fish sandwich all are one to two servings from the meat, fish, and poultry group. One egg, a handful of dry beans, or two spoons full of

If you're not sure of the correct amount in a serving, ask an adult to help you.

peanut butter make a serving, too. It's not as difficult as it sounds to get all the servings you need from all the groups!

Mixed Foods

Many foods are called mixed foods. Mixed foods belong to more than one of the pyramid food groups. For example, pizza is a mixed food. It may have cheese, meat, vegetables, and bread all on one slice! Lettuce and tomato on a burger is another example of mixing vegetables, bread, and meat in one meal. When you eat mixed foods, you often get a variety of nutrients.

Using the Pyramid

Understanding the food pyramid can help you to build healthy eating habits. Many cereal boxes show the food pyramid on their side panels. Some restaurants picture the pyramid on their menus. Look for the food pyramid when you eat cereal or visit a restaurant.

Some restaurant menus—especially menus for children—show the food pyramid as a reminder to choose healthy meals.

There are four important ways to use the food pyramid:

1. Eat many different kinds of food.
2. Choose foods that are low in fat.
3. Don't eat too much sugar.
4. Eat plenty of vegetables, fruits, and grain products.

Following the advice in the food pyramid is a good way to be sure that you'll be healthy and strong.

Learning good eating
habits when you're young
can help you stay healthy
when you're an adult.

To Find Out More

Here are some additional resources to help you learn more about the food pyramid, healthy eating, and good nutrition:

 **Books**

Brooks, F. **Food and Eating.** EDC Publishing, 1989.

Kalbacken, Joan. **Food Safety.** Children's Press, 1998.

Kalbacken, Joan. **Vitamins and Minerals.** Children's Press, 1998.

Macmillan Children's Book Staff. **Food.** Knopf, 1997.

Patten, Barbara. **Nutrients: Superstars of Good Health.** Rourke, 1996.

Royston, Angela. **Healthy Me.** Barron, 1995.

Stille, Darlene R. **The Digestive System.** Children's Press, 1997.

Wake, Susan. **Vegetables.** Lerner, 1990.

Organizations and Online Sites

Food and Drug Administration (FDA)
5600 Fishers Lane
Rockville, MD 20857
http://www.fda.gov/

This government agency works to protect the health of the American people by making sure that food is safe, healthy, and clean.

Food Pyramid Guide
http://www.ganesa.com/ food/index.html

Presents a graphical representation of a balanced, healthy diet. Complete with a short description of each food group.

KidsHealth
http://www.kidshealth.org/

Created by medical experts, this site is devoted entirely to the health of children. Contains up-to-date information about growth, food, fitness, and lots of surprises!

National Institutes of Health (NIH)
9000 Rockville Pike
Bethesda, MD 20892
http://www.nih.gov/

A government agency, the NIH works to uncover knowledge that will lead to better health for all Americans. The NIH also sponsors research at laboratories, universities, medical schools, and hospitals.

United States Department of Agriculture (USDA)
14th Street and
Independence Avenue SW
Washington, DC 20250
http://www.nal.usda.gov/ fnic/Fpyr/pyramid.html

This is a group of federal agencies that work to ensure food safety and nutrition, to support American farming, and to conserve our country's natural resources and the environment.

Important Words

diet what you eat and drink

habit something that you do every day

level position in the food pyramid

nutrient parts of food that help you grow and stay healthy

product something that is made or grown

pyramid solid figure with a square base and four triangle-shaped sides that meet at their tops

variety many different foods

Index

Meet the Author

Joan Kalbacken lives in Normal, Illinois. A former teacher, she taught mathematics and French for twenty-nine years.

Ms. Kalbacken is the author of several books for Children's Press, including *Food Safety* and *Vitamins and Minerals*, companion books to *The Food Pyramid*. Ms. Kalbacken is also the recipient of a Distinguished Illinois Author Award from the Illinois Reading Council, and a Merit Teaching Award from the Illinois Those Who Excel Program.